CANCER HOROSCOPE & ASTROLOGY 2025

Mystic Cat

Suite 41906, 3/2237 Gold Coast HWY

Mermaid Beach, Queensland, 4218

Australia

islandauthor@hotmail.com

Copyright © 2024 by Mystic Cat

Time set to Coordinated Universal Time Zone (UT±0)

All rights reserved. This book or any portion thereof may not be reproduced or used in any manner without the publisher's express written permission except for the use of brief quotations in a book review.

The information accessible from this book is for informational purposes only. None of the data should be regarded as a promise of benefits. It should not be considered a statutory warranty or a guarantee of results achievable.

Images are used under license from Fotosearch & Dreamstime.

Contents

January   16
February   24
March   32
April   40
May   48
June   56
July   64
August   72
September   80
October   88
November   96
December   104

Hello there, lovely readers! Let me explain why my horoscope books may give different readings for each zodiac sign. The sky is always bustling with astrological activity, and I want to focus on what's most important for each star sign.

Every zodiac sign is unique, and the planets up above affect them differently. When I create horoscopes, I pay extra attention to the most critical astrological events for a specific sign. Some days, there might be lots of stuff happening in the stars, but one thing stands out as the essential factor for a particular zodiac sign.

I also consider which planet rules a sign and its associated element. This in-depth consideration helps me tailor my interpretations to match a sign's characteristics.

Ultimately, my goal is to provide you with unique advice and insights that match the cosmic influences for your sign. By focusing on what makes each sign special, I hope to help you understand yourself better and navigate the energies around you. Embracing your sign's strengths and challenges is the key to making my horoscopes feel uniquely aligned for you.

Cosmic Blessings,

Sia Sands

CANCER 2025
HOROSCOPE & ASTROLOGY

Four Weeks Per Month

Week 1 – Days 1 - 7

Week 2 – Days 8 - 14

Week 3 – Days 15 - 21

Week 4 – Days 22 – Month-end

CANCER

CANCER

Cancer Dates: June 21 to July 22

Symbol: Crab

Element: Water

Planet: Moon

House: Fourth

Colors: Silver

Cancer is the fourth astrological sign in the zodiac, falling under the Water element. Individuals born under the Cancer sign are known for their emotional sensitivity, nurturing nature, and intuitive abilities. The symbol of Cancer, the crab, represents protection, adaptability, and the connection between land and sea.

Cancer individuals possess solid emotional depth and the ability to empathize with others. They are naturally inclined to care for and nurture those around them, often creating a sense of emotional security for their loved ones. Ruled by the Moon, the planet of emotions and instincts, Cancerians are deeply in touch with their feelings and often rely on their intuition to navigate life.

Cancer is associated with home, family, and emotional foundations in the Fourth House of the Zodiac. This placement emphasizes Cancer's strong connection to their family and roots and desire to create a safe and harmonious home environment.

Silver is Cancer's color due to its associations with intuition, emotions, and lunar influences. This color reflects the reflective and empathetic qualities of Cancer individuals.

In summary, Cancer embodies emotional depth, nurturing, and intuition. Those born under this sign tend to be compassionate, protective, and devoted to their loved ones. Their strong connection to their emotions and their ability to provide comfort make them valuable sources of support in both personal and professional relationships.

The Chinese Zodiac is a system that assigns an animal sign to each year in a 12-year cycle, and each animal is associated with certain personality traits and characteristics.

The Year of the Snake, in particular, holds special significance within Chinese culture and is rich in symbolism.

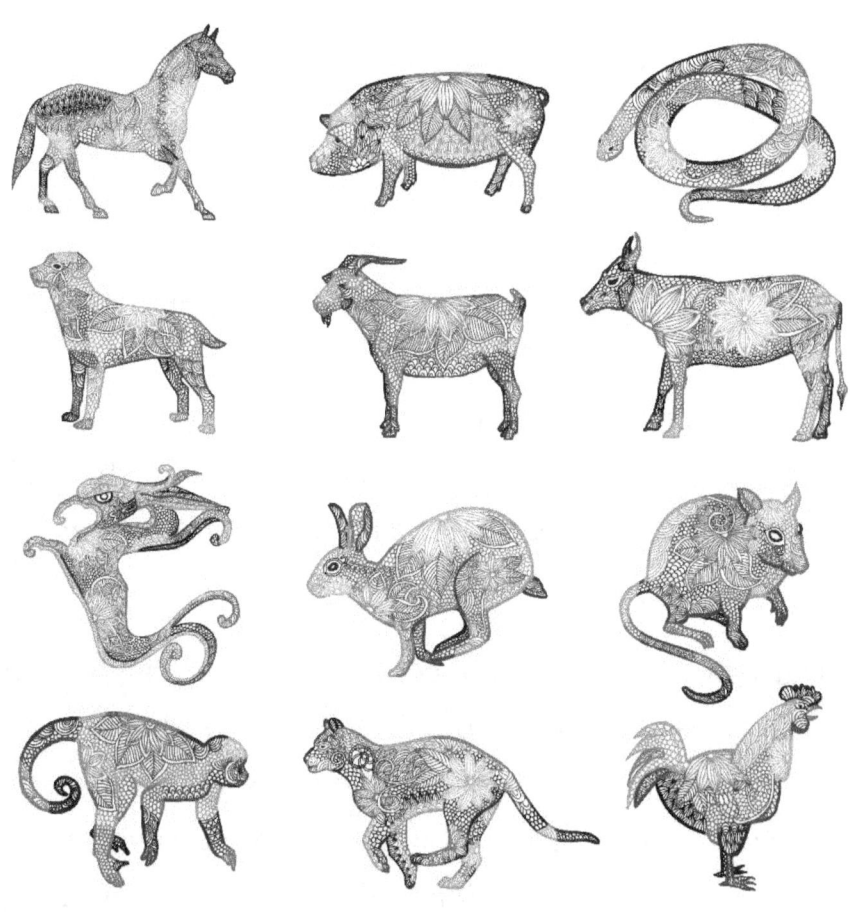

2025

The Chinese Year of the Snake

Cancer individuals are known for their nurturing, intuitive, and emotionally sensitive nature. They strongly connect to their emotions and prioritize their relationships and home life. When the Year of the Snake arrives, it introduces a blend of energies that can resonate deeply with the Cancer personality.

During this year, Cancer individuals might find themselves drawn to the Snake's qualities of introspection and transformation. Just as snakes shed their skin to grow, Cancer might embark on a journey of emotional growth and renewal, allowing them to let go of past burdens and embrace new beginnings.

The Year of the Snake encourages Cancer to delve further into its intuitive side. It's a time for them to trust their gut feelings and navigate their lives based on their inner wisdom. Just as snakes sense their environment, Cancer individuals could find themselves more attuned to the emotional undercurrents around them.

Cancer's nurturing nature aligns well with the Snake's ability to protect and provide. This year might inspire Cancer to focus on creating a secure and harmonious environment for themselves and their loved ones, much like the Snake's role as a guardian.

The Year of the Snake could encourage Cancer to deepen their emotional connections in relationships. Just as snakes rely on their senses to understand their surroundings, Cancer might seek to understand others' feelings on a profound level, fostering intimacy and empathy.

While Cancer individuals are known for their sensitivity, the Year of the Snake invites them to explore their inner world even more deeply. It doesn't mean becoming overwhelmed by emotions; instead, it's about embracing personal growth through self-reflection and understanding.

Ultimately, the Year of the Snake offers Cancer individuals emotional renewal and deeper connections. By tapping into the Snake's symbolism of shedding the old and embracing the new, Cancer can release emotional baggage and nurture meaningful relationships that align with its intuitive and caring nature.

CANCER 2025 HOROSCOPE & ASTROLOGY

JANUARY WEEK ONE

As the Moon gracefully steps into Capricorn, you'll feel a distinct shift in your emotional landscape. Capricorn's energy brings a sense of discipline and ambition to the forefront of your emotions. You'll find yourself focused on your long-term plans and ambitions, ready to tackle challenges with a determined spirit.

Now, hold onto your cosmic seats because we've got a New Moon in the mix! It's like the universe handing you a fresh canvas and a palette of possibilities. This New Moon invites you to set intentions, particularly regarding your career and public image. Think about where you want to climb that success ladder and what goals you're aiming for. Whether it's a new job, a big project, or even a fresh outlook on your professional life, this is your cosmic reset button.

As the Moon glides into Aquarius, you're in for a shift towards an independent and innovative emotional vibe. Aquarius' energy is like a cosmic rebel, encouraging you to break free from the norm and embrace your individuality.

JANUARY WEEK ONE

Brace yourself for a cosmic wave of romance and dreamy vibes as Venus gracefully waltzes into Pisces. This celestial tango adds a touch of enchantment to your love life and personal style.

Buckle up, cosmic voyagers, because when Mars locks horns with Pluto, it's like a high-octane showdown between the cosmic gladiator and the underworld's enigma. Your desires burn with an intensity that could rival the Sun, but beware of power struggles and hidden agendas lurking in the shadows.

As the Moon pirouettes gracefully into Pisces, your emotions take on a fluid, dreamlike quality. It's inviting you to explore the realms of intuition and imagination.

When the Sun forms a harmonious sextile with Saturn, it's like the universe giving you a well-deserved pat on the back. This celestial handshake brings a sense of stability and accomplishment to your endeavors.

Get ready for an energetic cosmic gearshift as the Moon charges into Aries. No ordinary celestial transit; it's like a heavenly lightning bolt igniting your passion.

JANUARY WEEK TWO

☼ As Mercury gracefully enters Capricorn, it ushers in a pragmatic and systematic approach to communication and thought. Your mental landscape becomes focused on the long term, making this a perfect time to strategize goals and engage in serious, structured conversations.

☾ The Moon dances into lively Gemini, infusing your emotions with curiosity and sociability. This celestial transition sparks your desire for intellectual exploration and engaging conversations. It's as if the universe encourages you to pick up the phone, initiate discussions, and soak knowledge like a cosmic sponge.

☾ But wait, the Moon has more in store as it continues its journey into nurturing Cancer. Emotions take center stage, and you'll find yourself drawn to the warmth of home and the embrace of family. Wrap yourself in the comforting blanket of home and let those you love know how much they mean to you.

♂ Meanwhile, Mars forms a harmonious trine with Neptune, infusing actions with enchantment. This cosmic collaboration sparks your inner artist.

JANUARY WEEK TWO

⚡ The Sun shares a harmonious trine with Uranus, electrifying your world with innovation and a hunger for change. The universe encourages you to embrace new experiences and unconventional ideas. It's a cosmic green light for personal growth, so don't be afraid to venture into uncharted territory.

🌕 Then, as we bask in the glow of the Full Moon, your achievements and goals take center stage. This lunar spectacle marks a culmination of your efforts, inviting you to celebrate your successes and assess your life's direction. It's a moment of clarity and revelation under the Moon's illuminating gaze.

🌙 The Moon continues its celestial voyage, now landing in Leo's dramatic realm. It's your cosmic cue to take the stage and share your radiant energy with the world.

✦ Venus squares off with Jupiter, creating an appetite for indulgence and pleasure. While it's essential to savor life's finer things, remember to exercise moderation during this aspect. It's like a cosmic buffet, offering an abundance of delights.

JANUARY WEEK THREE

◐ The opposition between the Sun and Mars sets the cosmic stage for a dynamic clash of wills. Your assertiveness and desires may face challenges and conflicts. It's a celestial tug-of-war, urging you to balance ambitions and the need to cooperate with others.

☽ With the Moon's transition into Virgo, this cosmic shift encourages a focus on self-improvement and efficient organization, making it an ideal time for tending to daily tasks and responsibilities.

⚡ The Sun's harmonious sextile with Neptune infuses life with creativity. You'll find it easier to tap into and express your artistic side during this celestial alignment.

💜 Venus's conjunction with Saturn brings commitment to your relationships and values. It's as if the cosmic lovebirds are making a long-term pact, emphasizing the importance of stability and maturity in heart matters.

☽ As the Moon gracefully moves into Libra, your emotional focus shifts towards balance and harmony in your interactions with others.

JANUARY WEEK THREE

Mercury's sextile with Saturn enhances your communication skills and organizational abilities. It's a cosmic green light for structured thinking and effective planning, helping bring your ideas to practical fruition.

Mercury's sextile with Venus adds a touch of charm and diplomacy to your conversations and social interactions. You'll find it easier to express your feelings and connect with others on an emotional level during this cosmic embrace.

With the Sun's transition into Aquarius, you'll embrace a more unconventional and progressive mindset. Celebrating your uniqueness and engaging in forward-thinking endeavors is a cosmic invitation.

The Sun's conjunction with Pluto brings a powerful surge of transformation and rebirth. It's as if you're undergoing a cosmic metamorphosis, shedding old layers and embracing your inner strength.

As the Moon later enters Scorpio, your emotions take on an intense quality. You explore the hidden and delve into matters of significance during this cosmic phase.

JANUARY WEEK FOUR

⚡ When Mars forms a harmonious sextile with Uranus, you're infused with dynamic energy and an appetite for change. It's like a cosmic call to action, encouraging you to embrace innovation and assert your individuality.

🗣 Mercury's opposition to Mars sets the stage for assertive communication but may also lead to conflicts.

☽ Mercury's trine with Uranus sparks inventive thinking and a thirst for knowledge.

☽ As the Moon gracefully transitions into adventurous Sagittarius, you'll experience a desire for exploration and a broader perspective. Your emotional landscape expands, inviting you to embrace new experiences and ideas.

💜 Venus forming a trine with Mars ignites passion and harmony in your relationships. It's a cosmic dance of love and desire, fostering affectionate connections.

🌑 Mercury's sextile with Neptune adds a touch of enchantment to your thoughts and communication. Your imagination soars, and you'll find it easier to express your ideas with a creative and empathetic flair.

JANUARY WEEK FOUR

🗣 Mercury's transition into innovative Aquarius opens the door to forward-thinking ideas and a desire for intellectual freedom. Your mind thrives on diversity.

✺ Mercury's conjunction with Pluto marks intense intellectual exploration and transformation. It's like a cosmic deep dive into the mysteries of the mind, urging you to uncover hidden truths.

● The New Moon heralds a fresh beginning, a cosmic canvas for setting intentions and manifesting desires.

⚡ Uranus turning direct signals a shift in cosmic energy, encouraging you to embrace change and innovation with renewed enthusiasm.

☽ The Moon's transition into intuitive Pisces enhances your emotional sensitivity and connection to the unseen realms. It's a time to engage in soulful reflection.

✷ The Sun's trine with Jupiter brings optimism and expansion. You can pursue goals and enjoy the cosmos' support. It's a time to harness the expansive energy of Jupiter and let it carry ambitions to new heights.

FEBRUARY WEEK ONE

💜 When Venus aligns harmoniously with Neptune, it's as if a celestial symphony serenades your heart. Love and romance take on an enchanting and ethereal quality, urging you to embrace your inner poet and express your affections with artistic flair. During this magical alignment, your emotions are infused with sensitivity and compassion, making it time for deepening connections and exploring the mystical aspects of love.

🌙 As the Moon gracefully enters the fiery realm of Aries, your emotions ignite with passion and assertiveness. It's like a cosmic adrenaline rush, propelling you to take on new challenges and boldly initiate projects.

○ Mercury's harmonious trine with Jupiter amplifies your communication skills and intellectual pursuits. Your mind is a treasure trove of expansive ideas, and conversations flow with optimism and wisdom.

🌙 As the Moon moves into the sensual terrain of Taurus, your emotions find solace in simplicity and stability. You'll take comfort in life's earthly pleasures, relishing in the sensory experiences that bring serenity.

FEBRUARY WEEK ONE

🐏 With Venus's dynamic ingress into Aries, your love life and personal style receive a bold and independent makeover. You may take the lead in matters of the heart, pursuing your desires with fearless determination. This celestial energy empowers you to embrace individuality and make courageous romantic choices.

⏩ Jupiter's direct motion signals a period of forward momentum and expansive growth. Projects and plans that may have been on hold can now progress with renewed vigor. As expansion opportunities abound, it's as if the cosmic winds are propelling you toward goals.

🌙 The Moon's transition into chatty Gemini infuses your emotional landscape with curiosity and sociability. It's an ideal time for networking and engaging in intellectually stimulating exchanges.

💜 Venus's sextile with Pluto adds depth and intensity to your relationships and desires. This passionate and transformative energy invites you to explore the profound connections and hidden desires within your heart's sanctuary. It's a cosmic invitation to embrace the transformative power of love.

FEBRUARY WEEK TWO

As the Moon gracefully enters the nurturing embrace of Cancer, your emotions take on a sensitive and caring quality. You'll find comfort in the familiar and seek solace in the warmth of home and family. This cosmic shift encourages you to prioritize emotional well-being and connect with your inner circle.

A harmonious alignment occurs as the Sun and Mercury combine forces, infusing your thoughts and communication with radiant clarity. Your words shine brightly, and your mind is sharp. It's an excellent time for self-expression, sharing ideas, and engaging in meaningful conversations.

Mars forms a constructive trine with Saturn, providing a steady and disciplined approach to your goals and ambitions. This cosmic alliance empowers you to channel your energy into long-term projects with focus and determination.

As the Moon moves into confident Leo, your emotions exude charisma and self-assuredness. It's as if you're ready to take center stage, and you'll be drawn to activities that allow you to showcase your unique talents.

FEBRUARY WEEK TWO

⚡ The Sun's square to Uranus electrifies your life with unpredictability and the desire for freedom. It brings an urge to break free from routine or embrace unconventional ideas. This cosmic aspect encourages you to embrace change and listen to your inner rebel.

🌕 The Full Moon illuminates your accomplishments and emotional fulfillment. It's a time to celebrate your achievements and release what no longer serves your well-being, creating space for new beginnings.

🌙 The Moon's transition into meticulous Virgo encourages practicality and attention to detail. You'll find satisfaction in organizing your surroundings and focusing on tasks that require precision and efficiency.

🌑 On Valentine's Day, Mercury gracefully enters the dreamy waters of Pisces, infusing your thoughts and conversations with empathy and imagination. During this cosmic phase, your communication style becomes more intuitive and compassionate. It's a beautiful time to express your feelings and connect deeply and emotionally with others.

FEBRUARY WEEK THREE

☽ With the Moon gracefully pirouetting into Libra, the cosmic spotlight shines on harmony and balance in your life. Emotions take on a refined and diplomatic tone, making it an ideal time for smoothing out any relationship wrinkles. Use this lunar energy to cultivate peace and fairness in your interactions, and you'll find that compromising and finding common ground become second nature.

☽ Later, as the Moon plunges into intense Scorpio, your emotional landscape takes a profound turn. Under this cosmic influence, your feelings dive deep, seeking to explore the hidden realms of your psyche. IEmotional authenticity becomes paramount during this lunar phase, and you may find that you're more in tune with the unspoken nuances of your own and others' feelings.

☉ The Sun's transition into compassionate Pisces marks the beginning of a season saturated with heightened sensitivity and artistic inspiration. Under the influence of this empathetic and imaginative energy, you'll feel a connection to the collective consciousness and the unspoken currents of emotion that flow in.

FEBRUARY WEEK THREE

The Moon's journey into adventurous Sagittarius encourages you to embrace optimism and expand your horizons. It's as if the universe is urging you to set your sights on new horizons, metaphorically and literally. You'll be drawn to novel experiences, diverse cultures, and philosophical insights. This lunar phase sparks a thirst for knowledge and a yearning for freedom, igniting your wanderlust and encouraging you to seek out new frontiers in the world or within your beliefs.

Mercury's square with expansive Jupiter creates a dynamic interplay of ideas and communication. While this alignment can infuse your conversations with enthusiasm and a sense of possibility, navigating it with awareness is essential. It's easy to become swept up in the grandeur of your visions, but remember to ground your expansive thinking with a dose of practicality. Be cautious about overcommitting or making promises that might be challenging to keep. This aspect encourages you to balance visionary thinking and the pragmatism needed to turn those visions into reality.

FEBRUARY WEEK FOUR

As the Moon gracefully steps into steadfast Capricorn, your emotional landscape takes on a pragmatic and disciplined tone. This lunar influence encourages you to prioritize your long-term goals and ambitions. You'll find satisfaction in setting clear objectives and taking incremental steps toward your aspirations. Emotionally, you may gravitate towards structure and responsibility, seeking a sense of accomplishment through your actions and decisions.

Mars, the planet of action and motivation, turns direct, infusing your endeavors with newfound energy and momentum. It's as if a cosmic roadblock has been removed, allowing you to move forward with determination and clarity. Your passions and desires regain their strength, propelling you toward your goals with renewed vigor.

As the Moon transitions into open-minded Aquarius, your emotions take on an innovative and free-spirited quality. You'll be drawn to unconventional ideas, social causes, and unique perspectives. This lunar phase encourages you to connect with a diverse range of people and embrace your individuality.

FEBRUARY WEEK FOUR

The Moon's ingress into compassionate Pisces invites you to dive into the depths of your emotions and intuition. This sensitive lunar phase fosters empathy and creativity, making it an ideal time for artistic expression and spiritual exploration. You'll feel a stronger connection to the collective consciousness; your dreams and visions may hold significant insights.

Mercury's sextile with Uranus adds an element of excitement and intellectual stimulation to your conversations and mental processes. Your mind is open to innovative ideas and unconventional solutions. This cosmic alignment encourages you to think outside the box. It's a favorable time for brainstorming, technological advancements, and exploring concepts.

The New Moon marks a fresh beginning and an opportunity to set new intentions. During this lunar phase, you have the cosmic support to plant the seeds of your desires and goals. It's a time for introspection, setting intentions, and visualizing your future. Consider what you'd like to manifest and embark on this new lunar cycle with purpose and optimism.

MARCH WEEK ONE

☾ Venus, the planet of love and harmony, embarks on a retrograde journey. During this period, your relationships and values may undergo a reevaluation. It's a cosmic invitation to revisit the past, reassess your desires, and reflect on matters of the heart. This retrograde phase encourages you to explore the depth of your affections and consider what truly brings you joy and fulfillment in your connections with others.

☿ Mercury's conjunction with dreamy Neptune adds a touch of mysticism and creative inspiration to your thoughts and communication. Your imagination takes flight, and you may find it easier to express yourself through art, poetry, or spiritual discussions. This cosmic alliance encourages you to embrace your intuition and engage in empathetic and compassionate conversations.

⚡ The Sun's square with Jupiter brings a sense of optimism and expansion. While you may feel inspired to pursue grand plans and adventures, balancing enthusiasm and practicality is vital. Be mindful of overindulgence or excessive optimism. This aspect encourages you to dream big while maintaining a grounded approach to your aspirations.

MARCH WEEK ONE

☽ As the Moon transitions into sensual Taurus, your emotions take on a more grounded and practical tone. You'll find comfort in life's simple pleasures, from savoring delicious meals to enjoying the touch of nature. Emotionally, stability and security become paramount, and you may seek to create a harmonious environment that nurtures your senses.

☽ When the Moon moves into inquisitive Gemini, your curiosity and desire for social interaction are amplified. Your mind becomes agile, and you're drawn to conversations and activities stimulating your intellect. This lunar phase is excellent for learning, networking, and engaging in lighthearted communication.

☿ Mercury's sextile with transformational Pluto adds depth and intensity to your conversations and thought processes. This celestial fusion encourages you to delve fearlessly into the profound realms of intellectual exploration. Your words carry a transformative power, and you're drawn to investigate complex subjects and uncover hidden truths.

MARCH WEEK TWO

☺ The harmonious trine between the Sun and Mars infuses your actions with vitality and determination. Your energy is high, and you're driven to pursue your goals enthusiastically and confidently. This cosmic alignment empowers you to take assertive steps toward your ambitions, making it a favorable time for initiating projects and asserting your willpower.

☾ As the Moon enters spirited Leo, your emotions take on a dramatic and expressive flair. You'll feel a strong desire to shine and be recognized, making it a perfect time to embrace your creativity and share your talents with the world. Your inner performer comes to life during this lunar phase.

💬 Mercury's conjunction with Venus adds a touch of charm and eloquence to your communication. Your words are imbued with grace and appeal, making it an ideal time for sweet conversations and expressions of affection. It's a cosmic invitation to engage in harmonious discussions and connect with others on a deeper, more meaningful level.

MARCH WEEK TWO

◯ The Sun's conjunction with Saturn marks a period of discipline and a strong sense of responsibility. This cosmic alignment encourages you to establish a solid foundation for your ambitions and take a mature approach to your endeavors.

◉ The Full Moon shines a spotlight on your achievements and projects. It's a time to celebrate your progress and acknowledge your hard work. This lunar phase may also bring a culmination of efforts and a clearer sense of direction for the future.

⚡ The Sun's sextile with Uranus adds a touch of excitement and innovation to your life. While it can lead to unexpected developments, it's also an opportunity to break free from limitations and embrace change. This cosmic aspect encourages you to welcome the unconventional and explore new horizons.

☽ As the Moon enters harmonious Libra, your emotions gravitate towards balance and harmony in your relationships. You'll seek cooperation and fulfillment in creating an atmosphere of peace and understanding. It's a time to find compromises in your interactions.

MARCH WEEK THREE

🔄 Mercury's retrograde journey begins, leading you into a period of reflection and reevaluation. This cosmic retreat is an excellent time to review your plans, revisit past decisions, and refine your communication. Be patient and prepared for possible delays in travel and technology, and double-check essential details.

☽ As the Moon gracefully enters Scorpio, your emotions take on an intense quality. It's a time of emotional transformation and introspection, making you more inclined to explore your innermost feelings and the mysteries of life. Trust your intuition during this lunar phase. This lunar phase encourages you to explore the secrets within yourself and the world around you. You may find a heightened sense of intuition and a desire to uncover hidden truths.

♐ Later, the Moon transitions into adventurous Sagittarius, igniting your optimism and curiosity. You'll be drawn to explore new horizons, engage in philosophical discussions, and seek adventures. Your adventurous spirit is highlighted during this lunar influence.

MARCH WEEK THREE

☀ When the Sun conjuncts Neptune, the boundary between reality and dreams blurs, allowing for heightened intuition, creativity, and spiritual experiences. It's a time to connect with your inner mystic, indulge in artistic pursuits, and tap into the collective unconscious.

☺ With the Sun's entrance into Aries, the astrological New Year begins with the Vernal Equinox. It marks a time of renewal and a fresh start. Aries energy is bold, and you'll feel a surge of vitality and courage, making it an excellent period for taking the initiative and pursuing your goals. The energy of Aries encourages fresh starts and a pioneering spirit. As the days grow longer, you'll feel a surge of vitality and a desire to take the lead in your endeavors.

☽ Venus' sextile with Pluto adds depth and intensity to your relationships and desires. This cosmic connection encourages profound emotional experiences and transformation in heart matters. You may find yourself drawn to passionate and transformative connections and the exploration of your innermost desires.

MARCH WEEK FOUR

☾ As the Moon gracefully moves into the steadfast sign of Capricorn, your emotions take on a more practical and disciplined tone. The universe urges you to roll up your sleeves and focus on your responsibilities and long-term goals. During this lunar phase, you'll feel satisfied tending to your duties and embracing your inner ambition.

♣ The Sun's conjunction with Venus sets the stage for a harmonious dance of love and affection in your life. It's as if the cosmos is spotlighting your relationships and all that brings you joy. During this time, your interactions are filled with tenderness and an appreciation for the beauty surrounding you. It's the perfect moment to express your feelings and revel in the finer details of existence.

✦ The Sun's sextile with Pluto deepens your experiences, inviting transformation and empowerment into your world. This alignment encourages you to dive beneath the surface, uncover hidden truths, and create meaningful change. You'll be able to tap into your inner strength and embrace growth.

MARCH WEEK FOUR

● The New Moon marks a fresh beginning and an opportunity to set new intentions. This lunar phase invites you to plant the seeds of your desires and envision the future you wish to create. It's a moment of renewal and a cosmic blank canvas on which to paint your aspirations.

☿ Mercury's entrance into Pisces enhances your intuition and empathy in your communications. Your words take on a compassionate and poetic quality, making it an ideal time for deep, heartfelt conversations. You'll discover a natural ability to connect with others on a profound level.

♆ With Neptune's entry into Aries, a new era of dreams and spiritual exploration dawns. This cosmic shift may inspire innovative and idealistic visions for the future, fostering a sense of renewal and individuality.

☽ As the Moon moves into the practical and sensual sign of Taurus, your emotions turn toward comfort and security. Stability and sensuality are paramount during this lunar phase, inviting you to revel in the tangible delights of existence.

APRIL WEEK ONE

When Saturn forms a sextile with Uranus, the cosmic energies align to promote positive change and innovation. This harmonious aspect encourages you to blend tradition with modernity, offering unique opportunities for progress within established structures. It's a time to embrace new approaches while respecting the wisdom of the past.

Mars's sextile with Uranus ignites your passions and desire for adventure. This cosmic combination sparks your adventurous spirit and encourages you to take bold actions in pursuit of your goals. Expect the unexpected and be open to exciting new opportunities.

Mars's trine with Saturn lends a disciplined and focused energy to your endeavors. It's as though you have the stamina and determination to tackle even the most challenging tasks. This aspect provides the endurance to bring your long-term plans to fruition.

As the Moon enters radiant Leo, your emotions take on a more dramatic and expressive quality. This lunar phase encourages self-expression and creative pursuits.

APRIL WEEK ONE

☼ The Sun's sextile with Jupiter radiates optimism and opportunity. This cosmic alignment brings a sense of expansion and abundance to your life. It's a favorable time for personal growth, setting ambitious goals, and confidently embracing new experiences.

💖 Venus's trine with Mars creates a harmonious dance of love and desire. Your relationships benefit from a blend of passion and affection, making it an ideal time for romantic connections. This aspect fosters harmony, improving your ability to express your love.

💑 Venus's conjunction with Saturn emphasizes commitment and responsibility in your relationships. It's a period when you may take your partnerships more seriously and seek stability and longevity. This alignment encourages you to address any challenges.

☿ Mercury's direct motion shifts your mental clarity and communication. After introspection and review, you'll find it easier to make decisions and confidently express your thoughts. This change is an opportune time to move forward with your plans and projects.

APRIL WEEK TWO

✧ The sextile between Venus and Uranus introduces an element of surprise and delight into your love life and creative pursuits. Your relationships may take unexpected turns, filled with exciting adventures and unconventional experiences. This aspect encourages you to break free from routine and embrace the beauty of bizarre self-expression forms. It's a time when your unique qualities are appreciated, and you draw people who celebrate your individuality.

☽ When the Moon transitions into Virgo, you become attuned to the finer details of your daily life. Your emotions find solace in order and efficiency. This lunar phase is like a cosmic invitation to declutter your emotional space and focus on practical matters. You may desire to organize your surroundings.

♥ As the Moon glides into Libra, the atmosphere is imbued with a desire for harmony and balance. This lunar phase encourages you to seek peace in your relationships and surroundings. You are diplomatic, eager to mend any conflicts, and foster a sense of unity. Beauty and aesthetics become paramount during this period, and you may be drawn to art, music, and design.

APRIL WEEK TWO

The Full Moon illuminates the culmination of your efforts and intentions. It's a time of reflection and celebration. You'll reap the rewards of your hard work and commitment. Emotions run high during this phase, allowing you to release what no longer serves you and embrace the achievements you've attained. It's a potent time for making decisions and letting go of the past.

With Venus turning direct, the areas of your life connected to love, relationships, and aesthetics begin to regain their natural flow. Any challenges or stagnation you've experienced in these areas are gradually lifted. If there were any unresolved issues in your relationships, you now have the opportunity to address them with a fresh perspective.

The Moon's shift into Scorpio adds a layer of intensity and depth to your emotions. It's a time when you're drawn to explore the mysteries of life and your psyche. Your intuition is heightened, guiding you to uncover hidden truths and delve into your emotional depths. This phase encourages introspection and the courage to confront aspects of your inner world that may have been previously uncharted.

APRIL WEEK THREE

◊ With Mercury's entrance into bold and fiery Aries, your communication style becomes assertive and direct. This placement fosters a pioneering spirit in your thoughts and ideas, making it an excellent time to start new projects or share your innovative concepts.

🌑 When Mercury aligns with dreamy Neptune, your mental landscape takes on a surreal and imaginative quality. It's like a cosmic poet's pen, allowing you to weave words and ideas into beautiful, ethereal tapestries. This aspect encourages creativity, intuition, and empathy in your communication. You may find yourself drawn to artistic or spiritual pursuits, using language to evoke emotions and inspire others.

🦁 Mars's ingress into bold and confident Leo infuses your actions with passion and a desire for recognition. You're unapologetically assertive about pursuing your goals. This placement encourages you to take center stage and express your individuality with flair. Your creative energy surges, making it an ideal time to showcase your talents and pursue projects that ignite your passion.

APRIL WEEK THREE

Easter Sunday symbolizes rebirth and renewal, symbolizing the emergence of light and hope. It's a time for reflection, forgiveness, and celebrating new beginnings.

When Mercury forms a sextile with transformative Pluto, your communication becomes profound and insightful. It's as if you have a heightened ability to penetrate beneath the surface and uncover hidden truths. This aspect encourages deep and meaningful conversations that can lead to personal growth and transformation. Your words carry a weight of influence, making it a favorable time for research, psychological insights, or strategic planning.

As the Moon moves into independent and forward-thinking Aquarius, you may feel drawn to social causes and group activities. This lunar phase fosters a sense of camaraderie and a desire to make a positive impact.

When the Sun forms a square with Mars, there's a surge of dynamic energy that can lead to assertiveness and even conflict. This aspect encourages you to channel your energy constructively rather than impulsively.

APRIL WEEK FOUR

☾ The Sun's square to Pluto is a celestial tug-of-war that stirs up intense power dynamics and personal transformations. This aspect challenges you to confront deep-seated fears and hidden desires, ultimately leading to personal growth and empowerment. It's a time to face the shadows within and emerge stronger.

💔 Venus's conjunction with Saturn casts a pragmatic tone over your relationships and artistic endeavors. This alignment encourages commitment and responsibility in matters of the heart. While it may feel heavy, it provides the foundation for lasting and mature connections.

🔥 As the Moon charges into Aries, you're in for an energetic shift. This cosmic spark ignites your passion and drive. Your emotions are bold and spontaneous, and you can take action and initiate new projects.

♂ Mars opposing Pluto sets the stage for a cosmic showdown between the warrior and the underworld. This intense aspect can lead to power struggles and conflict, but it also provides the courage and determination to face formidable challenges. It's a time for transformation and the potential for rebirth.

APRIL WEEK FOUR

♣ When the Moon enters Taurus, your emotions find stability and a deep connection to the material world. This lunar phase inspires a sense of security and a desire for financial and emotional strength.

● The New Moon marks a fresh beginning, a cosmic blank slate to inscribe your intentions and dreams. It's a potent time for setting goals, initiating projects, and manifesting your desires. Use this lunar phase to plant the seeds and embrace the growth potential.

▪ As the Moon enters Gemini, your emotions take on a more curious and communicative tone. This cosmic planetary ingress is when you're drawn to social interactions, intellectual pursuits, and various interests. It's like a cosmic invitation to explore the world of ideas and engage in lively conversations.

☼ Venus's ingress into Aries adds a touch of excitement and spontaneity to your relationships and creative pursuits. It's like a cosmic declaration of independence, encouraging you to be more assertive in matters of the heart and infuse your artistic expression with a bold, individualistic flair.

MAY WEEK ONE

💗 The conjunction of Venus and Neptune creates an aura of enchantment in your love life and creative endeavors. It's as if a touch of magic graces your relationships and artistic expressions. This aspect fosters deep emotional connections and a heightened appreciation of beauty and sensuality. You're inclined to see the world through a more romantic and idealistic lens.

🦁 As the Moon moves into Leo, your emotions take on a more vibrant and expressive quality. It's like a cosmic stage where you shine with creativity and desire recognition. This lunar phase encourages you to indulge in enjoyable activities, seek the spotlight, and pridefully express your individuality.

🔄 When Pluto turns retrograde, it's a cosmic signal to journey into the depths of your transformation. This period prompts you to revisit and reflect upon the inner changes you've been undergoing. It's a time for introspection and reevaluating power dynamics in your life. You have the opportunity to release what no longer serves your personal growth.

MAY WEEK ONE

📖 Mercury's sextile with Jupiter enhances your communication skills and intellectual horizons. It's like a cosmic green light for learning, teaching, and sharing knowledge. This aspect promotes optimism, a broad perspective, and a love for exploration. You're open to new ideas and have a gift for conveying them in an inspiring way.

🌙 As the Moon enters Virgo, your emotions take on a practical and analytical tone. It's a time when you're inclined to pay attention to details and focus on tasks that require precision. This lunar phase encourages efficiency and a desire to improve your daily routines.

💜 Venus's sextile with Pluto electrifies your relationships with passion and intensity. This cosmic connection allows for profound emotional experiences and transformations in heart matters. You're more open to exploring the depths of your relationships and uncovering hidden desires. This aspect fosters a sense of empowerment and a deeper understanding of your desires and your partner's. The sextile between Venus and Pluto adds depth and passion, inviting you to explore the profound aspects of love and art.

MAY WEEK TWO

✻ When the Moon gracefully enters Libra, your emotions are attuned to harmony, balance, and social connections. This lunar phase encourages you to seek peace and beauty in your surroundings and relationships. You may yearn for diplomacy and fair interactions, and your artistic sensibilities are heightened.

✻ Mercury's entrance into Taurus brings a down-to-earth and practical tone to your thoughts and communication. You're inclined to express your ideas with patience and determination, making this an excellent time for planning, financial matters, and enjoying life's simple pleasures. This transit encourages you to communicate with stability and a systematic approach, making it an excellent time for planning and making sound decisions.

✻ As the Moon dives into Scorpio, your emotions take on an intense quality. You're drawn to probing beneath the surface and exploring hidden truths. This lunar phase encourages self-discovery and transformation, allowing you to release emotional baggage and heal.

MAY WEEK TWO

○ The Full Moon is a culmination of energies and a release time. It's like the climax of a cosmic story, where you see the results of your intentions and efforts from the previous New Moon. This lunar aspect is a decisive phase for letting go of what no longer serves you and embracing what you've manifested. It's a time to acknowledge your achievements and release what no longer serves you. This lunar phase fosters heightened emotions and a deeper understanding of your desires.

☿ Mercury's square to Pluto ignites profound and intense thoughts and conversations. This aspect encourages you to delve into the depths of your mind and examine the underlying motivations behind your ideas. It's a time for research, psychological insights, and the potential for transformative communication.

♐ When the Moon shifts into Sagittarius, your emotions are guided by a quest for adventure and knowledge. You're eager to explore new horizons, both mentally and physically. This lunar phase encourages spontaneity, optimism, and a desire for broader experiences.

MAY WEEK THREE

🌑 As the Moon gracefully enters Capricorn, your emotions take on a responsible and ambitious tone. You're driven to achieve your goals and take a structured approach to life. This lunar phase encourages discipline and focusing on long-term success, but balancing your commitments with self-care is essential.

☀ The Sun's conjunction with Uranus marks a dynamic and unpredictable moment. This celestial event can bring surprises and sudden insights that spark innovation and change in your life. It's a time when you're more open to experimentation and breaking free from the status quo.

👤 Mercury's square with Mars ignites your mental energy and communication but can lead to impulsive or hasty exchanges. It's essential to be mindful of your words and actions during this aspect to avoid conflicts or misunderstandings. Use this fiery energy to tackle intellectual challenges with enthusiasm. It's when you're passionate about your ideas but may need to manage impatience.

MAY WEEK THREE

🌑 As the Moon shifts into Aquarius, your emotions take on an independent and progressive quality. You're drawn to unconventional ideas and enjoy connecting with like-minded individuals. This lunar phase encourages you to embrace your uniqueness and explore innovative solutions to problems.

🕐 The Sun's sextile with Saturn brings a sense of stability and productivity to your endeavors. You're more focused on your responsibilities and long-term goals, making this an excellent time for planning and achieving results through disciplined efforts.

🌙 When the Moon enters Pisces, your emotions become dreamy and compassionate. It's when you're in touch with your intuition and creativity, making it ideal for artistic pursuits or acts of kindness. This lunar phase encourages you to connect with your spiritual side.

☀ The Sun's move into Gemini marks a more intellectually curious and communicative phase. You become eager to learn, share ideas, and engage in conversations. This solar shift encourages versatility and adaptability, making it easier for you to connect.

MAY WEEK FOUR

💜 Venus's trine with Mars brings a harmonious blend of passion and desire to your relationships and creative endeavors. It's as if the cosmic stage is set for harmony and cooperation between the masculine and feminine energies within you. This aspect encourages a balance of assertiveness and receptivity in matters of the heart.

☀ The Sun's sextile with Neptune infuses your life with magic and inspiration. Your intuition is heightened, and you're more attuned to the subtle energies surrounding you. This aspect encourages creativity, compassion, and a sense of spiritual connection.

🔺 When the Sun forms a harmonious trine with Pluto, it's like a cosmic invitation to transform and regenerate. This aspect empowers you to release old patterns and embrace your inner power. It encourages profound self-discovery and the ability to manifest your desires.

⚪ Mercury's conjunction with Uranus electrifies your thinking and communication. You're open to innovative ideas and may experience flashes of insight. This aspect encourages originality, change, and a desire to break free from mental constraints.

MAY WEEK FOUR

🪐 Mercury's sextile with Saturn enhances your ability to focus and plan. It's like a cosmic organizer, helping you precisely structure your thoughts and communications. This aspect supports long-term goals and responsible decision-making.

🌑 The New Moon marks a fresh beginning and an opportunity to set new intentions. It's like a cosmic reset button, allowing you to plant the seeds of your desires. This lunar phase encourages introspection and the formulation of new goals.

🔍 Mercury's trine with Pluto intensifies your mental processes and analytical abilities. You're drawn to deep and transformative conversations, and your insights are profound. This aspect encourages in-depth research and the ability to uncover hidden truths.

☀️ The Sun's conjunction with Mercury amplifies your communication skills and mental acuity. It's a time when your words carry weight and you can express yourself clearly. This aspect supports intellectual endeavors and effective self-expression.

JUNE WEEK ONE

☽ When the Moon gracefully enters Virgo, your emotions take on a practical and analytical tone. You become detail-oriented and focused on the finer points of life. This lunar phase encourages you to organize your surroundings, pay attention to your health, and seek a sense of order and efficiency in your daily routines.

☽ As the Moon moves into Libra, your emotions seek harmony and balance. You're more attuned to the needs of others and inclined to foster cooperation and diplomacy in your relationships. This lunar phase encourages you to find common ground and create a sense of beauty and peace in your interactions.

☽ Venus sextile Jupiter is a harmonious aspect that brings a touch of abundance and joy to your relationships and finances. Your social life may flourish, and you're likely to experience pleasant interactions with others. This aspect encourages generosity, optimism, and the pursuit of your desires. Your interactions are filled with warmth and generosity, making it an excellent time for social activities, romance, and artistic expression.

JUNE WEEK ONE

Mercury sextile Mars ignites your mental and communicative energies. You're filled with a sense of determination and enthusiasm, making it an excellent time for taking action on your ideas and plans. This aspect encourages assertive and direct communication.

Venus's ingress into Taurus brings a sensual and earthy quality to your relationships and pleasures. You're more inclined to savor life's simple and sensory pleasures, such as good food, comfort, and physical touch. This transit encourages stability and a deeper connection to your values and desires.

When the Moon moves into Scorpio, your emotions take on an intense and transformative hue. You may be more discerning and wise regarding hidden emotions and motivations. This lunar phase encourages introspection and a willingness to let go of what no longer serves you. You're drawn to explore the depths of your psyche and may engage in introspection and self-discovery. This lunar phase encourages transformation and a desire to uncover hidden truths and mysteries.

JUNE WEEK TWO

✷ When Mercury conjuncts Jupiter, your mind expands, and your thoughts become filled with optimism and possibilities. This aspect is like a burst of intellectual energy, encouraging you to dream big, share your ideas, and engage in meaningful conversations. You'll find it easier to grasp complex concepts and see the big picture.

♋ Mercury's ingress into Cancer marks a shift towards more emotionally driven and intuitive communication. Your thoughts may become intertwined with your feelings, and you'll seek more profound connections with others. This transit encourages nurturing conversations and empathetic exchanges.

☐ Mercury square Saturn creates a challenge in communication and mental processes. It may feel as though you're navigating mental roadblocks or encountering resistance in your discussions. While this aspect can bring a harsh tone to your thoughts, it also encourages you to approach problems with patience and a structured mindset.

♐ As the Moon moves into Sagittarius, your emotions take on an adventurous and free-spirited quality.

JUNE WEEK TWO

Venus square Pluto ignites intensity in your relationships and desires. It's a passionate and transformative aspect that may bring power struggles to the forefront. While challenging, it encourages you to delve into the depths of your emotions.

Jupiter's ingress into Cancer signals a shift towards nurturing and expansion within the family and emotional realms. You'll find joy and growth through connecting with your roots and creating a sense of home. This transit encourages you to embrace emotional well-being and seek abundance in your personal life.

The Full Moon is a culmination of energies, highlighting the completion of a lunar cycle. It's a time for reflection, closure, and the release of what no longer serves you. This lunar phase encourages you to let go of the past and acknowledge your achievements.

Mercury sextile Venus brings a harmonious blend of communication and affection. It's an excellent time for expressing love and appreciation to others, enhancing your charm and social interactions. Your words and gestures convey warmth and grace.

JUNE WEEK THREE

⚡ Mars square Uranus brings a burst of electric and unpredictable energy to your actions and desires. It's like a cosmic lightning strike, shaking up your routines and prompting you to break free from limitations. While this aspect can be impulsive, it also encourages you to embrace innovation and courage in pursuing your goals.

♃ Jupiter square Saturn sets the stage for a balancing act between expansion and limitation. You might feel torn between the desire for growth and the need for discipline. This aspect encourages you to find a harmonious middle ground where you can set realistic goals and work steadily toward your ambitions.

☾ As the Moon gracefully moves into Pisces, your emotions take on a dreamy and empathetic quality. This lunar phase fosters compassion, intuition, and a desire to escape into the world of imagination.

♂ Mars's ingress into Virgo brings a practical and detail-oriented approach to your actions. You'll be driven to tackle tasks with precision and efficiency, paying attention to the more minor aspects of your projects. This transit encourages using energy wisely.

JUNE WEEK THREE

🚀 As the Moon enters Aries, your emotions gain a burst of passionate and assertive energy. You'll feel more courageous and ready to take on challenges. This lunar phase encourages you to assert your individuality and take action on your desires with enthusiasm.

🪐 Jupiter square Neptune brings a clash between your idealism and your sense of reality. It's like a cosmic tug of war between dreams and practicality. This aspect encourages you to find a way to balance your spiritual aspirations with the need to stay grounded and realistic.

♣ When the Moon moves into Taurus, your emotions take on a stable and earthy quality. You'll seek comfort, security, and sensual pleasures. This lunar phase encourages you to connect with nature, enjoy delicious meals, and create a harmonious environment.

☀ The Sun's ingress into Cancer marks the June Solstice, a significant turning point in the year. It's a time of celebrating the longest day and the arrival of summer in the Northern Hemisphere. Cancer's energy encourages nurturing, home life, and emotional connections with loved ones.

JUNE WEEK FOUR

🚀 Mars sextile Jupiter is like a cosmic rocket, boosting your energy and confidence. This harmonious aspect encourages you to take on challenges and pursue your goals with enthusiasm and optimism. It's a favorable time for expanding your horizons, whether through travel, education, or other adventurous endeavors.

☼ When the Sun squares Saturn, it's a cosmic reminder of responsibility and limitations. This aspect can bring challenges and obstacles to your plans. It encourages you to take a realistic and disciplined approach to your goals, even if it feels like a temporary setback.

☾ Sun square Neptune is like a cosmic mist that blurs your focus and clarity. This aspect can bring confusion, doubts, or feelings of vulnerability. It encourages you to be cautious and discerning in your interactions and decisions, as things may not be as they appear.

🌱 Sun conjunct Jupiter is a burst of cosmic optimism and opportunity. This powerful aspect encourages growth, abundance, and a positive outlook on life. It's a time to expand your horizons, embrace new experiences, and tap into your inner wisdom.

JUNE WEEK FOUR

● The New Moon represents fresh beginnings and a clean slate. It's like a cosmic reset button, making it an ideal time to set intentions, start new projects, and initiate positive changes in your life. This lunar phase is all about planting the seeds of your desires.

● Mercury sextile Uranus brings inventive and forward-thinking energy to your communication and thought processes. This aspect encourages you to embrace change, innovative ideas, and open-minded discussions. It's a favorable time for creative problem-solving and expressing your unique perspective.

▲ Sun sextile Mars adds a boost of dynamic energy to your actions and initiatives. This aspect encourages assertiveness, courage, and a go-getter attitude. It's a great time to take action on your goals and assert your desires in a balanced and constructive manner.

● Mercury trine Saturn promotes structured and disciplined thinking. This aspect encourages practicality, attention to detail, and a systematic approach to your tasks and responsibilities. It's an excellent time for long-term planning and organization.

JULY WEEK ONE

🌑 As the Moon enters Scorpio, your emotions take on an intense quality. It's like a cosmic dive into the mysteries of your inner self. This lunar phase encourages introspection, transformation, and a desire to explore the hidden aspects of life.

⚡ Venus conjunct Uranus is a cosmic burst of excitement and change in your love and social life. It's like a lightning bolt of unexpected encounters and unconventional attractions. This aspect encourages you to embrace spontaneity and welcome unique experiences in relationships.

♊ Venus's move into Gemini brings a light and playful energy to your romantic and social interactions. It's like a cosmic breeze that encourages curiosity and versatility in your connections. This transit promotes lively conversations, a variety of interests, and a love of intellectual stimulation.

🔄 Neptune turning retrograde invites you to revisit your dreams and ideals. It's like a cosmic pause in the dreamy, imaginative realm, encouraging a deeper exploration of your fantasies and creative visions.

JULY WEEK ONE

☾ Venus sextile Neptune infuses your relationships with compassion and a touch of enchantment. It's like a cosmic wave of empathy and understanding. This aspect encourages acts of kindness, artistic expression, and a deeper emotional connection with loved ones.

♐ The Moon's ingress into Sagittarius brings a sense of adventure and a yearning for freedom to your emotions. It's like a cosmic call to explore new horizons and embrace optimism. This lunar phase encourages you to seek knowledge, expand, and follow your passions.

✦ Uranus's ingress into Gemini marks a period of intellectual curiosity and innovation. It's like a cosmic awakening of the mind, encouraging you to explore fresh ideas and communication methods. This transit may bring surprising changes in your thinking and a desire to break free from mental constraints.

♥ Venus trine Pluto deepens your emotional connections and enhances your passions. It's like a cosmic force of transformation in your love life, encouraging profound and intense experiences. This aspect promotes solid emotional bonds.

JULY WEEK TWO

🌙 With the Moon's ingress into Capricorn, a sense of responsibility and ambition takes center stage in your emotional landscape. It's as if a cosmic mentor has arrived, encouraging you to approach your feelings with a structured and disciplined mindset. During this time, you may find yourself more focused on your goals and obligations, seeking to achieve a sense of order and accomplishment in your life.

🌕 The Full Moon, with its radiant glow, marks a pivotal moment in your emotional journey. It's like a celestial spotlight shining on your achievements, desires, and lingering emotions. This phase serves as a cosmic mirror, inviting you to reflect on your progress, celebrate your successes, and release what no longer serves you. It's a time for closure and the culmination of energy.

🌙 As the Moon transitions into Aquarius, a spirit of independence and innovation infuses your emotional experiences. It's akin to a cosmic maverick awakening within you, urging you to explore unconventional avenues in your vibrant life. During this phase, you may feel drawn to unique and progressive ideas, as well as nurturing your social connections.

JULY WEEK TWO

Saturn's retrograde journey signifies a period of introspection regarding your responsibilities and long-term aspirations. It's as if a wise cosmic teacher has asked you to review the blueprints of your life. You are prompted to ensure that your ambitions align with your authentic desires and values. This introspective phase encourages you to make any necessary adjustments to create a solid foundation for your future.

With the Moon's entry into Pisces, your emotions take on a dreamy and empathetic quality. It's as if a cosmic artist has dipped their brush in the colors of the imagination and painted your emotional landscape with vivid, ethereal hues. During this phase, you may find yourself drawn to introspection, seeking a deep connection with your inner world, and fostering compassion for others.

This week's celestial transitions provide you with a diverse array of emotional experiences. From the pragmatic and responsible Capricorn to the liberating and innovative Aquarius and the dreamy and compassionate Pisces, each phase offers a unique perspective on your inner world.

JULY WEEK THREE

When the Moon gracefully enters Aries, you're greeted with a surge of dynamic energy that feels like a cosmic call to action. Your emotions take on an assertive and adventurous hue, encouraging you to embrace your inner pioneer. This lunar phase sparks the fires of initiative and enthusiasm within your heart, motivating you to explore uncharted emotional territories.

With Mercury turning retrograde, the cosmic messenger initiates a period of introspection, inviting you to revisit and review your thoughts, communication, and the way you engage with the world. It's akin to a celestial pause button, offering you a chance to reflect on past conversations, reconsider ideas, and fine-tune your mental processes. During this phase, the universe encourages you to embrace the art of self-expression and to clear up any lingering misunderstandings, fostering a greater sense of clarity in your interactions.

As the Moon gracefully moves into Taurus, a soothing sense of stability washes over your emotional landscape. This lunar placement acts like a cosmic anchor, providing security rooted in the material world.

JULY WEEK THREE

♥ When Mercury forms a harmonious sextile with Venus, your thoughts and feelings engage in a beautiful dance of synergy. It's as if your mind and heart are in perfect alignment, facilitating sweet and meaningful communication. This celestial connection fosters tender conversations and heartfelt expressions of love, making it an ideal period for connecting with others on a deeper emotional level. Your words are like a soothing balm, creating harmony and understanding in your relationships.

☽ The Moon's transition into Gemini infuses your emotions with a delightful sense of curiosity and communication. It's akin to a cosmic storyteller awakening within you, encouraging you to share your feelings, thoughts, and ideas with the world. This lunar phase amplifies your intellectual curiosity and fuels a desire to engage in lively conversations with those around you. Your ability to connect and communicate with others shines brightly during this time, and you may find yourself drawn to engaging dialogues and the exchange of ideas.

JULY WEEK FOUR

☀ When the Sun gracefully moves into Leo, it's like a cosmic spotlight shining on your inner performer. Leo, the zodiac's royal sign, inspires you to embrace your creativity, confidence, and innate leadership abilities. During this solar transit, you'll radiate warmth and charisma, drawing others into your magnetic orbit.

☀ The Sun's harmonious sextile with Uranus ushers in an electrifying and innovative energy. It's as if the universe hands you a ticket to the cosmic carnival, where you can explore uncharted territory and embrace your individuality with enthusiasm. This aspect encourages you to think outside the box, sparking creative insights and potentially leading to unexpected but exciting experiences.

☀ The Sun's harmonious trine with Saturn brings a stabilizing and disciplined influence to your life. It's like a cosmic mentor applauding your efforts and offering you a steady hand of support. This aspect encourages you to set practical goals, follow through with your commitments, and establish a strong sense of self-discipline. You'll find that your ambitions are met with success and recognition.

JULY WEEK FOUR

🌑 The New Moon marks the beginning of a fresh lunar cycle. It's a cosmic reset button, allowing you to set new intentions and plant the seeds for your future. The New Moon invites you to embrace new beginnings and start afresh in various areas of your life.

☉ When the Sun opposes Pluto, it's like a cosmic showdown between the luminary of self-expression and the planet of transformation. This aspect can bring power struggles and challenges to the forefront. It encourages you to confront issues related to control, authority, and personal transformation.

❀ Venus's graceful transition into Cancer brings a nurturing and emotionally sensitive energy to your relationships. During this time, you'll seek emotional connection and security in your partnerships. You may find comfort in expressing your affections and creating a haven for love to flourish.

☉ The Sun's conjunction with Mercury aligns your thoughts and self-expression in a harmonious dance. It's like a cosmic conversation between your intellect and your core identity.

AUGUST WEEK ONE

💔 When Venus forms a square aspect with Saturn, it's as if the cosmic stage is set for a challenging act in the theater of love and responsibility. This aspect creates a tug-of-war between your desires for romance and your need for structure and boundaries. You might find yourself wrestling with feelings of restriction and limitations within your relationships. It's essential to strike a delicate balance between your emotional needs and the practical commitments you've made. While this aspect can present obstacles, it also offers an opportunity to strengthen your bonds by demonstrating commitment and working through challenges.

🌙 Venus square Neptune adds a layer of dreamy confusion to the intricate dance of your heart. It's akin to navigating through a mist of illusions and fantasies, where what you desire might not align with reality. This aspect can lead to misunderstandings or the tendency to idealize someone or a situation, potentially setting you up for disappointment. It's crucial to trust intuition, remain cautious about making impulsive decisions, and take a grounded approach to relationships, ensuring your emotions are rooted in truth.

AUGUST WEEK ONE

♐ With the Moon's ingress into Sagittarius, your emotional landscape takes on an adventurous and free-spirited hue. It's as if your heart is set on a quest for exploration, both in the external world and within your inner realm. During this lunar phase, your emotional well-being thrives on embracing a broader perspective.

♑ As the Moon journeys into Capricorn, a grounded and pragmatic emotional energy prevails. This lunar placement encourages you to find fulfillment in accomplishing tasks, making progress in your career, and tending to your worldly duties. There's a sense of satisfaction in putting in the effort to reach your goals.

♎ Mars's entrance into Libra ushers in a desire for equilibrium and diplomacy in your actions. It's akin to being guided by the scales of justice as you yearn for harmony and fairness in your interactions. During this cosmic shift, you're more inclined to approach conflicts with a sense of grace and cooperation. Your efforts to create peace and maintain balance in your relationships are supported, making it an excellent time to work together to find mutually beneficial solutions.

AUGUST WEEK TWO

♎ The opposition between Mars and Saturn introduces a contrasting, somewhat challenging theme. It's like a cosmic tug-of-war between your desire for freedom and the need for structure and responsibility. You might encounter obstacles and delays in your pursuit of personal goals. Yet, this aspect also serves as a valuable reminder to take a measured, strategic approach to your endeavors. It's a time for patience and systematic planning.

🌕 The Full Moon is a powerful culmination of emotional energy. This phase marks the peak of the lunar cycle when the Sun opposes the Moon, highlighting the tension between your conscious desires (the Sun) and your emotions (the Moon). It's a time of heightened emotions, clarity, and revelations. You may gain insights into your deepest needs and desires, which can guide your future actions.

♂ Mars's opposition to Neptune brings a dreamy, somewhat elusive quality to your actions. It's like navigating through a foggy realm where reality and fantasy blur. This aspect invites you to align goals with your ideals and to trust your intuition.

AUGUST WEEK TWO

Mercury turning direct marks a shift in communication and thought processes. It's as if the cosmic gears are moving forward after a period of reflection and reassessment. Clarity returns, and you can move forward with plans and decisions that may have been on hold during Mercury's retrograde phase.

Saturn's sextile to Uranus blends the energies of tradition and innovation. It's like a cosmic handshake between the old and the new. This aspect encourages you to find innovative solutions within the framework of established structures. You can introduce positive changes stably and constructively, creating lasting and meaningful progress.

The conjunction of Venus and Jupiter is a harmonious meeting of two benevolent planets, bringing joy, love, and abundance. It's as if the universe is showering you with blessings in matters of the heart and personal fulfillment. This aspect invites you to celebrate love, enjoy life's pleasures, and expand your social connections. It's a time when luck and positivity flow your way, so seize the moment to enjoy the fun of life.

AUGUST WEEK THREE

⚡ When Mercury forms a harmonious sextile with Mars, it's like a celestial collaboration of mental prowess and assertive communication. Your thoughts and words become a dynamic force, poised with purpose and precision. This cosmic synergy allows you to tackle tasks that demand mental acuity and a proactive approach with finesse. Whether you're planning a project, engaged in intensive problem-solving, or simply having a heart-to-heart, you'll find that your words carry an extra weight of influence.

🌙 As the Moon gracefully glides through the realm of curious Gemini, your curiosity flourishes, and your intellectual horizons expand. It's as if a gentle cosmic breeze sweeps through your mind, clearing the cobwebs and creating an open space for the exploration of new information and ideas. This lunar influence is a breath of fresh air for your intellectual pursuits, making it the perfect time to dive into stimulating discussions, immerse yourself in books, courses, or workshops, and relish the diversity of knowledge that surrounds you.

AUGUST WEEK THREE

✦ The encore presentation of Mercury's sextile to Mars is akin to a cosmic high-five, reinforcing mental acumen and assertive communication. This aspect is your trusty companion in the realm of decision-making and interaction, empowering you to articulate your thoughts with conviction and clarity. It's a mental powerhouse that excels in problem-solving, allowing you to cut through mental obstacles like a hot knife through butter.

☽ When the Moon enters the tender realm of Cancer, emotions swell to the surface. It's as if a soothing cosmic lullaby encourages you to connect with your feelings and those of others. This lunar placement creates an atmosphere of emotional nurturing, where you may feel more inclined to express your care and affection for loved ones. Home and family take on added significance during this time, making it ideal for cozy gatherings and heartfelt conversations.

✻ The Moon's journey through dramatic Leo adds a touch of theatricality to your life's stage. This lunar influence encourages you to embrace your inner artist. So, let creativity flow, and let your light shine! 🎭

AUGUST WEEK FOUR

☼ As the Sun gracefully enters Virgo, you may feel a shift in your focus and priorities. This transit encourages practicality, attention to detail, and a desire to organize your life. It's an excellent time for getting things in order, setting new routines, and focusing on health and well-being.

● With the New Moon, you're standing at the threshold of new beginnings. This lunar phase is like a blank canvas, offering you the opportunity to set intentions, make plans, and initiate projects. It's a time of fresh starts and planting the seeds for your future endeavors.

⚡ When the Sun forms a challenging square with Uranus, you might experience a sense of restlessness and a desire for change. This aspect can bring unexpected events or the need to break free from routine. Embrace innovation and flexibility during this period.

💜 Venus's move into Leo infuses your relationships with warmth and passion. You may seek appreciation, admiration, and creative expressions of love. Your social life can become more vibrant and enjoyable.

AUGUST WEEK FOUR

💔 Venus's harmonious trine with Saturn encourages stability in your relationships. It's a favorable aspect for making commitments and strengthening the bonds you share with others.

✦ The sextile between Venus and Uranus brings excitement and novelty to your love life and social interactions. Be open to unique experiences and spontaneous connections.

☽ Venus's trine with Neptune adds a touch of romance and fantasy to your relationships. This aspect fosters compassion, empathy, and a deeper emotional connection with your loved ones.

💔 Venus's opposition to Pluto can stir up intense emotions and power struggles in your relationships. It's a time for introspection and transformation but also for handling these challenges with care and understanding.

🌠 The sextile between Uranus and Neptune encourages spiritual insights and creative inspiration. This transit is a time for exploring the mystical and imaginative aspects of life.

SEPTEMBER WEEK ONE

🍃 As Saturn gracefully glides into Pisces, a profound shift occurs in the cosmos. Your focus turns inward, and you become more attuned to your emotional depths. Pisces' influence encourages you to explore your dreams, emotions, and spiritual side. It's a time for heightened intuition and empathy, where you'll find solace in compassion and understanding. Use this period to dive into your inner world, rekindle your connection to the mystical, and gain a more profound sense of purpose.

📄 Mercury's entrance into Virgo adds a touch of practicality to your thought processes. This transit sharpens your analytical skills and attention to detail. It's an ideal time to get organized, plan your daily routines, and focus on matters related to health and wellness. Virgo's precision and systematic approach help you sort through the finer points of life.

⚡ When Mercury forms a square with Uranus, prepare for a jolt of mental energy and potential flashes of insight. This aspect stimulates innovative thinking and a desire for change. Your mind might feel a bit restless, but this restlessness can lead to creative breakthroughs.

SEPTEMBER WEEK ONE

The square between Mars and Jupiter ignites a fire within you, fueling a desire for growth and adventure. You're filled with energy and enthusiasm, ready to tackle your goals and ambitions. However, be cautious not to take on too much at once. To make the most of this energetic blend, channel it wisely and focus on what truly matters to you.

As Uranus turns retrograde, you're encouraged to embark on an internal journey of reflection. This retrograde period prompts you to review the changes and innovations you've experienced in recent months. It's a time for integrating newfound insights and embracing a deeper understanding of your unique path to personal liberation.

The Full Moon marks a high point in the lunar cycle, illuminating your accomplishments and intentions set during the previous New Moon. Emotions can run high, so use this phase for introspection, self-awareness, and releasing what no longer serves you. It's a potent moment to assess your progress and make adjustments as needed. The cosmos is your guide on this transformative journey.

SEPTEMBER WEEK TWO

🌙 When the Moon ushers in Aries, a burst of dynamic energy surges through your emotions. You'll feel invigorated and assertive, eager to take the lead and tackle challenges head-on. It's a period ripe with opportunities to initiate new projects and assert your individuality. Your emotional landscape becomes charged with enthusiasm, making it an ideal time to kick-start endeavors that have been on your mind.

🌙 As the Moon glides into Taurus, a sense of groundedness envelops your emotional state. During this phase, you prioritize comfort, security, and life's tangible aspects. Additionally, financial matters may come into focus, and this lunar shift provides a steady backdrop for addressing them with prudence and care.

☀ The Sun's harmonious sextile with Jupiter brings a wave of optimism and opportunity into your life. This cosmic alignment expands your horizons, both mentally and physically, and encourages you to step boldly into the world. It's a time when setting ambitious goals, pursuing your dreams, and seeking new adventures are infused with confidence and positive energy. This aspect acts as a guiding star, illuminating your path forward.

SEPTEMBER WEEK TWO

With the Moon's entrance into Gemini, your curiosity and sociability take center stage. This lunar transition creates an atmosphere of lightness and mental agility.

Mercury's sextile with Jupiter further enhances your communication skills and intellectual prowess. Under this cosmic influence, your words carry weight, and your ideas have the power to inspire and uplift. It's a period tailor-made for making plans, embarking on educational pursuits, and sharing your insights with a broader audience. Your mental insight is in its prime, guiding you to explore the vast landscape of knowledge and personal growth.

When the Sun forms a conjunction with Mercury, your thoughts and self-expression meld seamlessly. This celestial partnership sharpens your intellect, enabling you to articulate your ideas with precision and confidence. Your mind is clear, and communication flows effortlessly. This period is marked by mental understanding and a strong connection between your inner thoughts and external words. It's an ideal time for meaningful conversations, decision-making, and productive mental endeavors.

SEPTEMBER WEEK THREE

✦ Venus, the planet of love and beauty, graces us with its energy in a harmonious sextile with passionate Mars. This celestial dance encourages romance, creativity, and the pursuit of desires. Your relationships are infused with harmony and sensuality, making it an ideal time to express your affections and connect with loved ones.

🗣 However, Mercury's opposition with stern Saturn may pose some communication challenges. Conversations could feel heavier, and misunderstandings may arise. This aspect calls for patience when sharing your thoughts and ideas.

☀ Mercury's entry into Libra, the sign of balance and diplomacy, shifts the focus toward harmonious interactions. During this period, you'll have a natural inclination to seek peace and fairness in your conversations, making it an excellent time to resolve conflicts and foster understanding.

🌊 On the flip side, Mercury's opposition with dreamy Neptune can cast a nebulous veil over your thought processes, leading to potential confusion or misunderstandings.

SEPTEMBER WEEK THREE

☿ Mercury's trines with Uranus and Pluto bring a wave of mental acuity and transformative insights. Your mind is sharp and adaptable, allowing you to break free from conventional thinking and embrace innovative concepts.

♥ Venus' entry into practical Virgo means you'll find joy in attending to the finer details of your connections, and a pragmatic touch may enhance your romantic life.

⚡ Yet, the square between Venus and Uranus introduces an element of unpredictability. You may experience unexpected changes in your relationships or find yourself drawn to unconventional romantic interests.

☀ The Sun's opposition with steadfast Saturn can present challenges related to self-expression and personal authority. It might feel like you're facing obstacles that require determination and patience to overcome.

● With the arrival of a New Moon, a fresh chapter begins, offering an opportunity to set intentions and embark on a journey of self-discovery and personal growth.

SEPTEMBER WEEK FOUR

◊ Mars's fiery entrance into Scorpio sets your life ablaze with renewed purpose and intensified passion. Your desires deepen, and you're willing to go to great lengths to pursue your goals. This cosmic alignment ignites your determination and drive, making it an excellent time to tackle challenges head-on. You're armed with a potent energy that can be harnessed for transformative growth.

☼ The September Equinox marks a pivotal moment in the year, signaling the transition from one season to another. It's not merely a celestial event but a reminder from the cosmos to seek balance in your life. Just as nature adapts to the changing seasons, you, too, must adjust to life's ever-evolving circumstances. It's a time for reflection, realignment with your goals, and finding equilibrium in the ebb and flow of existence.

♎ With the Sun's graceful ingress into Libra, the spotlight shines brightly on your relationships. The harmonious energy of Libra encourages you to seek balance and fairness in all your interactions. This period is ideal for mending imbalances in your connections, fostering a sense of equilibrium and understanding.

SEPTEMBER WEEK FOUR

⚡ The Sun's harmonious trines with Uranus and Pluto infuse your life with a potent blend of transformation and innovation. You become more receptive to change and open to new ideas and experiences.

☽ As the Moon gracefully transitions into Scorpio, the emotional depths beckon. Your feelings and motivations become shrouded in mystery, and you'll find yourself delving into your innermost self. It's a time for introspection, self-discovery, and understanding the driving forces behind your actions, providing a profound opportunity for emotional growth.

🗑 However, the square between Mars and Pluto can intensify power struggles and conflicts. Approach such situations with tact and a diplomatic touch. Avoid provoking confrontations, and instead, seek common ground to channel the powerful energies constructively.

🏔 The Moon's entry into Capricorn shifts your focus to ambition and long-term goals. The celestial energies support your efforts to achieve lasting success, provided you maintain discipline and a strong work ethic.

OCTOBER WEEK ONE

✳ When the Moon glides into Aquarius, the cosmic stage is set for a wave of intellectual excitement and an unquenchable thirst for freedom. You might find yourself drawn to unconventional ideas, advocating for humanitarian causes, or connecting with kindred spirits who share your progressive mindset. This lunar placement encourages community engagement and exploration of intellectual pursuits, and it's the perfect time to let your innovative spirit take the lead.

💬 However, as the week unfolds, a celestial showdown emerges. A square aspect between Mercury and Jupiter gives rise to a fascinating clash between intricate details and grand, expansive thinking. While the vast energy of Jupiter fills you with enthusiasm and big ideas, the precise and analytical nature of Mercury pushes you to pay attention to the nitty-gritty details.

🌙 Later on, when the Moon journeys into dreamy Pisces, your emotions take on a more sensitive, compassionate quality. The gentle waters of Pisces encourage you to explore your inner world and connect with the deeper layers of your emotions.

OCTOBER WEEK ONE

🕵 With Mercury's entry into Scorpio, your thoughts dive to greater depths. You become an intellectual detective, seeking the hidden truths and exploring the mysteries that lie beneath the surface. This ingress is a period of deep introspection and a strong desire to understand the intricate nuances of complex issues.

🌕 The Full Moon, a celestial spectacle, takes center stage, illuminating your path with its radiant glow. It is the culmination of the lunar cycle, a moment of realization and completion. It's a time to reflect on the intentions you set during the New Moon and observe how they have evolved and manifested. As you stand in the Moon's brilliant light, you're invited to release what no longer serves you and move forward with newfound clarity.

🌑 Nevertheless, a square between Mercury and Pluto adds a layer of intensity to your communication and thought processes. While you're determined and laser-focused, there's a risk of becoming fixated on ideas or getting entangled in power struggles. This aspect calls for a delicate balance between assertiveness and open dialogue, urging you to be mindful of peacekeeping.

OCTOBER WEEK TWO

✿ The harmonious sextile between Venus, the planet of love and beauty, and expansive Jupiter creates a cosmic symphony of warmth and abundance. Your social interactions are infused with generosity, and a spirit of camaraderie blossoms in your relationships. This celestial alignment encourages you to savor the richness of life and share it with those you cherish.

☽ Venus, now gracing Libra, engages in a cosmic dance of opposition with stern Saturn. This celestial tango prompts a careful balancing act in matters of love and aesthetics. Navigating the delicate interplay between desire and practical considerations becomes essential, calling for patience and diplomatic finesse.

☾ As the Moon flows into Cancer, a nurturing energy envelops you, fostering a deeper connection with your emotions. Home and close relationships take center stage, offering a comforting sanctuary. This lunar phase encourages you to attune to your feelings and create a harmonious space for emotional well-being.

♥ Venus, now elegantly placed in Libra, introduces an air of grace and charm to your interactions.

OCTOBER WEEK TWO

Pluto's direct motion signals a powerful cosmic shift, urging you to embrace transformative growth. It's a time to release old patterns and step into a renewed sense of self. The universe supports profound inner evolution during this period.

The Moon's entrance into Leo adds a radiant and theatrical flair to the cosmic stage. This cosmic ingress is your cue to express your authentic self boldly, embracing creativity and self-assurance.

Venus, engaging in a harmonious trine with innovative Uranus, injects a spark of excitement into your love life and creative endeavors. Embrace spontaneity and be open to unconventional expressions of affection.

Venus's trine with Pluto brings a depth of passion and intensity to your connections. This celestial alignment encourages transformative experiences in matters of the heart and creative pursuits. Venus's dance adds layers of warmth and enchantment. Venus brings excitement and depth to your experiences of love and creativity.

OCTOBER WEEK THREE

☽ As the Moon gracefully steps into meticulous Virgo, a sense of precision colors your emotional landscape. You may find solace in attending to details, organizing your surroundings, and embracing a practical approach to your feelings. It's a celestial nudge to nurture yourself through acts of service and mindful attention to the finer aspects of life.

☼ The cosmic stage sets for a dynamic interplay as the Sun squares Jupiter. This alignment prompts you to balance optimism with practicality. While expansive visions and grand ideas may capture your attention, the square encourages you to ground these aspirations in realistic plans, ensuring a harmonious fusion of dreams and tangible results.

☽ Moving into Libra, the Moon invites you to explore the beauty of balance and harmony in your emotional responses. Relationship dynamics take center stage during this lunar transition, urging you to seek equilibrium and cooperation. Embrace diplomacy, appreciate aesthetics, and find joy in shared experiences.

OCTOBER WEEK THREE

🌑 Mercury, the communicator, aligns with assertive Mars in a conjunction that sparks vibrant intellectual energy. Your thoughts and words gain a decisive edge, fostering effective communication. This cosmic synergy encourages directness and decisiveness in your verbal expressions and academic pursuits.

🌑 The arrival of the New Moon signals a cosmic reset, offering a blank canvas for new beginnings. It's a potent time to set intentions, initiate projects, or cultivate fresh perspectives. Allow the lunar darkness to inspire the birth of ideas and aspirations.

🌙 Transitioning into Scorpio, the Moon dives into the depths of emotions and psychological realms. This phase encourages introspection, unveiling hidden truths, and embracing the transformative power of vulnerability. Dive into the profound currents of your inner world, allowing emotional regeneration.

In this celestial dance, the New Moon marks a potent moment for fresh starts, and the lunar shift into Scorpio prompts introspection and emotional exploration.

🌑 🌙 ✦

OCTOBER WEEK FOUR

● The Sun's square with Pluto adds a touch of intensity to the cosmic narrative. This alignment brings forth a cosmic dance between the light of awareness and the shadows of the subconscious. It's an opportunity to confront power dynamics and embrace the process of regeneration, emerging more robust and authentic.

✻ Mercury's harmonious trine with expansive Jupiter opens the channels of communication and intellect. This cosmic alliance enhances your ability to think broadly and see the bigger picture. It's a time for positive exchanges of ideas and a broadening of your mental horizons.

✺ Mercury's trine with structured Saturn adds a touch of stability to the mental landscape. This alignment encourages disciplined thinking and strategic planning.

🚀 Mars' trine with Jupiter brings a surge of dynamic energy and enthusiasm. This cosmic alliance propels you forward, inspiring confidence and a can-do attitude. It's a time to take bold initiatives and expand your horizons with a sense of adventure.

OCTOBER WEEK FOUR

● Mercury's trine with Neptune creates a harmonious blend of intellect and intuition. This cosmic dance enhances your creative and imaginative faculties, allowing for inspired and visionary thinking. It's a time to trust your instinct and engage in artistic or spiritual pursuits.

♐ Mercury's ingress into Sagittarius adds a touch of adventurousness to your mental landscape. This planetary shift encourages a broader perspective and a thirst for knowledge. It's a time to explore new ideas, embrace diversity, and seek wisdom from diverse sources.

⌛ Mars' trine with Saturn adds a layer of practicality to your actions. This cosmic alignment supports disciplined and focused efforts, allowing you to make steady progress toward your goals. It's a time for planning and the implementation of strategies.

⚡ Mercury's opposition to Uranus brings a touch of unpredictability to the cosmic stage. This alignment may spark unexpected insights or disruptions in your thought patterns.

NOVEMBER WEEK ONE

Venus squares Jupiter, creating a cosmic tension between the planet of love and beauty and the planet of expansion and abundance. While this may evoke a desire for indulgence and pleasure, it's essential to find balance in your relationships and avoid overextending yourself. Be mindful of extravagance and prioritize authenticity in your connections.

Mars, the warrior planet, forms a harmonious trine with dreamy Neptune, infusing your actions with a touch of inspiration and creativity. This celestial alliance encourages a compassionate and imaginative approach to your pursuits. Consider incorporating your dreams and ideals into your ventures, allowing your actions to align with a higher purpose.

As Mars enters the adventurous realms of Sagittarius, the cosmic energy shifts towards exploration and expansion. A desire for freedom, growth, and a broader perspective fuels you. Embrace the adventurous spirit of Mars in Sagittarius as you embark on new journeys, whether physical or intellectual.

NOVEMBER WEEK ONE

🌖 The Full Moon graces the cosmic stage, illuminating the skies with its radiant glow. This lunar climax brings heightened emotions and a sense of completion. It's a time to release what no longer serves you and celebrate the achievements and lessons of the lunar cycle.

💀 Mars sextile Pluto intensifies the transformative potential of your actions. This cosmic alignment empowers you to make profound changes in your life, especially in areas where you've been seeking empowerment and regeneration. Use this energy wisely to foster positive transformations.

✨ The Moon, moving into the communicative realms of Gemini, encourages a more light-hearted and curious approach to your emotions. Engage in meaningful conversations, express your thoughts, and allow your mind to explore a variety of ideas.

💝 Venus gracefully enters the passionate and mysterious realms of Scorpio, deepening the intensity of your relationships. Dive into the depths of emotional connections, explore the mysteries of love, and embrace the transformative power of Venus in Scorpio.

NOVEMBER WEEK TWO

🌀 Embrace the celestial choreography as the revolutionary Uranus makes a groundbreaking entrance into Taurus. This cosmic shift heralds a period of innovation and upheaval in the realms of stability and security. It encourages you to adapt, welcoming unexpected changes with an open heart and a spirit of flexibility. The cosmic winds of change are blowing, urging you to explore and step into uncharted territory.

💔 Venus square Pluto adds a dramatic layer to the cosmic narrative, delving into the profound transformations within your relationships. This potent alignment acts as a cosmic alchemist, bringing deep-seated issues to the surface for resolution. It's an intense yet transformative phase, compelling you to confront challenges head-on and emerge stronger, wiser, and more attuned to matters of the heart.

🌙 As the Moon gracefully transitions into Cancer, the cosmic spotlight shifts to your emotional landscape. This nurturing energy prompts you to prioritize self-care and connect with your intuitive, feeling side. It's an invitation to seek solace in the comforts of home, fostering deeper connections with loved ones.

NOVEMBER WEEK TWO

Mercury, the cosmic messenger, embarks on its retrograde journey, inviting you to journey inward. This period encourages reflection and review, prompting a revisit of old projects, relationships, and unresolved matters. Exercise caution in communication, expecting delays and a revisiting of past narratives.

Jupiter, the expansive planet, takes a reflective pause as it turns retrograde. This cosmic realignment invites you to reassess your personal beliefs, philosophies, and growth goals. It's a time for inner exploration, refining your path, and aligning with a more authentic version of yourself.

Mercury's dynamic conjunction with Mars amps up the cosmic energy around communication and mental agility. Leverage this powerful synergy to express your thoughts assertively, tackle tasks with precision, and navigate challenges with strategic finesse. However, be mindful of potential conflicts arising from impulsive words.

NOVEMBER WEEK THREE

☼ The harmonious trine between the Sun and expansive Jupiter bathes you in an aura of confidence and optimism. It's as if the universe is encouraging you to dream big and embrace opportunities with enthusiasm. Your path is illuminated with a radiant glow, and the cosmos invites you to step into the spotlight of your potential.

⧗ The cosmic alliance of the Sun with Saturn brings a sense of stability and structure to your endeavors. It's a period where disciplined efforts can yield lasting results. Embrace responsibilities with a steady heart, and you'll find that the universe supports your journey towards long-term goals.

⟳ Mercury's sextile with transformative Pluto infuses your thoughts and communication with a profound depth. This celestial alignment invites you to explore the hidden realms of your mind, fostering powerful insights and meaningful conversations.

♏ As Mercury ventures into Scorpio, your mental landscape takes on a more intense and probing quality. Dive beneath the surface, uncovering hidden truths.

NOVEMBER WEEK THREE

● The New Moon marks a cosmic reset, inviting you to set intentions for the next phase of your journey. It's a potent moment for planting seeds of desire and envisioning the path ahead. Take a moment to reflect, release, and align with the energies of new beginnings.

◎ As the Sun aligns with Mercury in conjunction, your thoughts and self-expression take center stage. Your mind is sharp, and communication flows effortlessly. Use this time to articulate your ideas and engage in meaningful conversations.

♐ Mercury's transition into Sagittarius adds a dash of adventurous spirit to your mental pursuits. Your mind seeks broader horizons, and you're drawn to explore ideas that expand your understanding of the world. Embrace the joy of learning and sharing knowledge.

⚡ The Sun's opposition with Uranus introduces an element of unpredictability into your path. Embrace change with an open heart, and be willing to pivot in new and exciting directions. Flexibility is your ally during this dynamic celestial dance.

NOVEMBER WEEK FOUR

🌐 A celestial conversation between Mercury and Jupiter enhances your mental prowess and expands your intellectual horizons. Your mind is open to grand ideas, and you may find yourself drawn to learning or teaching on a broader scale. This alignment fosters positive thinking and the ability to see the bigger picture.

🏔 The Sun forms a harmonious sextile with Pluto, infusing your journey with transformative energy. This celestial aspect empowers you to tap into your inner strength and make positive changes in your life. You have the resilience to overcome challenges and the power to influence your circumstances. Embrace this cosmic support to delve into personal growth and embrace the potential for positive transformation.

💜 The merger of Mercury and Venus brings a touch of charm and eloquence to your communication style. This cosmic alliance enhances your ability to express love, beauty, and harmony. It's a favorable time for heartfelt conversations, artistic pursuits, and connecting with others on a deeper, more harmonious level. Let your words and expressions be a reflection of the beauty that surrounds you.

NOVEMBER WEEK FOUR

The cosmic messenger, Mercury, resumes its direct motion, lifting the fog of retrograde energies. Communication flows more smoothly, and any delays or misunderstandings begin to resolve. Use this time to move forward with plans, make decisions, and express your thoughts with increased clarity.

The ethereal trine between Venus and Neptune infuses your relationships and artistic endeavors with a touch of magic and inspiration. This celestial connection heightens your sensitivity to beauty and fosters a dreamy, romantic atmosphere. It's a beautiful time for creative expression, spiritual connections, and experiencing love on a soulful level.

Venus gracefully enters Sagittarius, adding a dash of adventurous energy to matters of the heart and pleasure. This cosmic shift encourages you to explore new avenues of love and enjoy life's joys with a sense of freedom and optimism. Embrace the spirit of adventure in your relationships and creative pursuits as Venus dances through the expansive and spirited sign of Sagittarius.

DECEMBER WEEK ONE

🌙 Embracing the cosmic shift, the Moon gracefully makes its ingress into Taurus, lending a touch of earthly sensuality to the emotional landscape. The energy becomes grounded and steadfast, encouraging a focus on comfort, stability, and the pleasures of the senses. This celestial transition prompts a time of nurturing emotions and indulging in life's simple yet gratifying pleasures.

💜 Venus, the cosmic enchantress, forms a harmonious sextile with Pluto, infusing relationships with intensity and transformative energy. This alignment invites a more profound connection, unveiling hidden desires and passions. The cosmic dance between Venus and Pluto encourages profound emotional experiences and the potential for positive transformations in matters of the heart.

🌙 As the Moon gracefully enters Gemini, the emotional atmosphere becomes more light-hearted and curious. Communication takes center stage, and there is a desire for variety and intellectual stimulation. This lunar transition encourages flexibility and adaptability.

DECEMBER WEEK ONE

The cosmos unveils the radiant glow of a Full Moon, casting its luminous energy across the celestial canvas. This decisive phase symbolizes culmination, completion, and a heightened emotional state. Emotions reach their peak, and intentions set during the New Moon now come to fruition. It's a time to reflect, release, and celebrate the abundance of the present moment.

Transitioning into Cancer, the Moon brings a nurturing and tender energy to the forefront. Emotional sensitivity deepens, fostering a connection to home, family, and personal security.

Mercury, the cosmic messenger, forms a harmonious trine with Neptune, the dreamy planet of inspiration. This celestial alliance enhances communication with a touch of poetic and compassionate flair. Imagination and intuition intertwine, making it a favorable time for creative expression, insights, and heartfelt connections.

Continuing its cosmic journey, the Moon gracefully steps into the radiant realm of Leo. Emotions take on a dramatic and expressive quality, and there's a desire for recognition and appreciation.

DECEMBER WEEK TWO

◊ Mars squares off against Saturn in a cosmic clash, demanding that you confront challenges with a balance of assertiveness and patience. It's a celestial lesson in strategic action, urging you to fortify your ambitions with a resilient and measured approach. Take each step with purpose, acknowledging that obstacles are stepping stones to success.

☽ As the Moon gracefully pirouettes into meticulous Virgo, the emotional landscape undergoes a shift toward practicality. This lunar phase encourages you to organize your thoughts and feelings.

◉ Neptune, the mystical planet, resumes its direct motion, lifting the veil on dreams and inspirations. What once seemed obscured gains clarity, and your inner visions become more lucid. Trust your intuition, for it is now a beacon guiding you through the realms of creativity and higher understanding.

⚡ Mercury, the messenger of the cosmos, engages in a dynamic dance of opposition with rebellious Uranus. This mental tango sparks innovative thoughts and unexpected mental breakthroughs.

DECEMBER WEEK TWO

📆 Mercury's harmonious trine with Neptune weaves a tapestry of enchantment into your communications. Your words become poetic vessels, carrying deeper meaning and resonating on a soulful level. Dive into creative expression, letting your imagination flow like a river of inspiration.

♐ Mercury boldly strides into adventurous Sagittarius, broadening the horizons of your thoughts. Your mind becomes a fearless explorer, venturing into uncharted territories of knowledge and wisdom. Embrace the thrill of curiosity and let intellectual wanderlust guide you.

♎ The Moon's ingress into Libra brings a sense of harmony to emotional realms. Relationships take center stage, and you're encouraged to seek equilibrium in your interactions. Embrace the beauty of fairness and cooperation, fostering connections that are both balanced and fulfilling.

✦ Mercury's harmonious sextile with transformative Pluto lends intensity and depth to your communications. Engage in meaningful conversations that have the power to catalyze profound changes.

DECEMBER WEEK THREE

♐ As Mars, the cosmic warrior, dons the disciplined robes of Capricorn, strategic energy infuses your actions. Channel this celestial support to pursue your ambitions with resilience. The cosmic battlefield becomes a training ground for focused efforts.

○ Saturn and the Sun engage in a celestial square, creating a cosmic tug-of-war between structure and self-expression. Challenges may arise, urging you to find a balance between your ambitions and the need for discipline. It's a call to assess the foundations of your goals and ensure they are built on solid ground.

♐ The Moon dances into expansive Sagittarius, setting the stage for a cosmic reset with the arrival of the New Moon. This celestial event marks a fresh beginning, inviting you to plant seeds of intention for the upcoming lunar cycle. Consider what you wish to manifest.

● The Moon gracefully glides into Capricorn, emphasizing the need for practicality and a disciplined approach to your emotions. Take a structured stance as you navigate the waters of your feelings, finding stability amid the tides.

DECEMBER WEEK THREE

● The elusive Black Moon enters the adventurous realms of Sagittarius, casting a mysterious aura over your aspirations. It's a time for exploring the unknown and embracing the wisdom that emerges from the shadows.

■ The December Solstice heralds a shift in cosmic energies as the Sun moves into Capricorn. It marks the longest night in the Northern Hemisphere, inviting you to reflect and set intentions for the coming months. It's a celestial turning point, symbolizing the return of the light and the promise of new beginnings.

♑ With the Sun's ingress into Capricorn, the cosmic spotlight now shines on your ambitions and goals. Take a practical approach to your aspirations, and let the wisdom of Capricorn guide grounded foundations.

☾ Sun squares off against Neptune, creating a celestial dance between reality and dreams. Navigate this energy with discernment, ensuring that your visions are grounded in practicality. Use the ethereal inspiration to fuel your creative pursuits.

DECEMBER WEEK FOUR

♥ As Venus engages in a cosmic waltz with Neptune, a sublime yet potentially complex energy envelops matters of the heart. The boundaries between reality and illusion may become hazy, prompting a need for careful discernment in your approach to relationships. Exercise caution against overly idealizing situations or individuals, and aim for clarity in your emotional connections.

✦ Venus gracefully transitions into the structured domain of Capricorn, imparting a sense of order and responsibility to your expressions of love and appreciation for beauty. During this phase, pragmatic considerations may influence your romantic pursuits, urging you to lay down robust foundations. Thoughtful acts of love could prove particularly effective in this period.

☾ The Moon glides into the ethereal waters of Pisces, beckoning you to delve into the poetic landscapes of emotion and intuition. This celestial alignment amplifies your sensitivity and compassion, creating an opportune moment for artistic endeavors, meditation, or introspective journeys to connect with your inner self.

DECEMBER WEEK FOUR

A shift in lunar energies unfolds as the Moon enters the bold domain of Aries. Feel the surge of initiative and a keen desire for action propelling you forward. Harness this dynamic force to confront challenges head-on and assert your individuality across various facets of life.

Continuing its celestial journey, the Moon moves into the grounded realms of Taurus. Immerse yourself in the pleasures of the material world, savoring and seeking solace in the stability of your surroundings.

Mercury engages in a celestial tussle with Saturn, creating a cosmic tension between communication and structure. This alignment calls for thoughtful and deliberate expression, yet be mindful of potential challenges or limitations in conveying your ideas. Exercise patience and diligence in your communication efforts, utilizing this time to refine your thoughts and concepts.

The Moon gracefully pirouettes into the inquisitive realms of Gemini, sparking intellectual curiosity and enhancing communication skills. Explore ideas and revel in the adaptability that this lunar phase brings.

NOTES

NOTES

NOTES

Astrology, Tarot & Horoscope Books.

Mystic Cat

www.ingramcontent.com/pod-product-compliance
Lightning Source LLC
LaVergne TN
LVHW051844080426
835512LV00018B/3056